I TOLD YOU SO

I TOLD YOU SO

WRITTEN BY:

DERRICK FLUELLEN JR.

FOREWORD BY:

RICHARD SPRAGGINS

I TOLD YOU SO

Copyright © 2022 Derrick Fluellen Jr.

All rights reserved.

ISBN: 9798590469543

I TOLD YOU SO

A message to the parents

Do you encourage or discourage your children when they talk about what they want to be in the future? If one of them was to come to tell you with big, wide, and remarkably anxious eyes and tell you that he or she wanted to be an actor on tv, would you suggest for your child to focus on something, say .... more **REALISTIC**? Well, if you do such a thing, then you are sending a clear message to your child that there are limitations to success.

We, as parents, should believe in the infinite potential of our youth. Our commitment is to provide them with the resources and support system that will· be necessary for them to realize and achieve their goals and dreams. As children, our greatest investment, we should encourage them to develop specific art forms, such as writing, acting, dancing, music, drawing, etc... Also, teach them to be responsible for the art forms' content, especially its ability to cause social change.

It amazes me how some of the youth that I have met maybe in their early teens but have a greater sense of what they want to do with their lives than some people I know who are in their 30's. Case in point, Derrick Fluellen knows exactly what he's going to do with his life, where he's headed, and how he will get there. After listening to him, I have learned a lot from him. Fact is, we can all learn from each other, young or old, and become more mature and develop a consciousness of how the world around us operates. At the same time, it is up to us as parents to understand our children, listen to them, and make time for them.

Hardly anyone these days take the time out to get into their world and learn them - not as a child - but as a person, which is the problem with most adults. They want to TELL them what to do instead of SHOWING them, and then subsequently expect immediate results. Showing a child takes time and a lot of patience. As a gardener of life, I continue to plant the seeds of life within these youth. With that comes patience because one that plants a seed today cannot expect a flower tomorrow.

As parents, it's a must that we have patience with our youth because if you pay attention, you'll see that in every child, there is a seed .... a seed of vast potential.

Remember the word YOUTH .... because the root word of it is YOU!!!

                                              Sincerely

                                          Richard Spraggins

I TOLD YOU SO

I TOLD YOU SO

DEDICATION

I DEDICATE THIS BOOK TO MY GREAT GRANDFATHER:

ERNESTO FLORES

SUNRISE: DECEMBER 7, 1938 – SUNSET: SEPTEMBER 10, 2020

YOU WERE A GREAT TEACHER AND A WONDERFUL INSPIRATION.
MAY YOUR SOUL REST IN PEACE.

I TOLD YOU SO

CONTENTS

ACKNOWLEDGMENTS i.

1 SEE IT ALL PG. # 1

2 YOU CAN LEARN A PG. # 5
LOT FROM A DUMMY

3 THE RICH MAN PG. # 7
&
THE BUILDER

4 BELIEVE IN YOURSELF PG. # 15

5 NEVER GIVE UP PG. # 18

6 THE RACE PG. # 21

7 THE AVENGERS PG. # 26

8 CRABS IN A BUCKET PG. # 30

9 MAKE A TURNAROUND PG. # 37
LIKE JUSTIN BIEBER

10 PRACTICE MAKES PERFECT PG. # 41

11 SHOOT FOR THE STARS PG. # 45

I TOLD YOU SO

I TOLD YOU SO

I TOLD YOU SO

ACKNOWLEDGMENTS

First, I would like to thank my mom and my dad for everything that you do. Thank you, Grandma, as well. I love all of my sisters to the bottom of my heart: Alayna, Mija, Ocira, and Hanna .... I love you! Thank you, Coach Styles, Coach Garcia, and Coach Wallace, for believing in me and making FOOTBALL so fun. Shout out to the whole team of PIRATES! Thank you, cousin, Twitche for being so cool, and that goes for all of my uncles and aunts as well. Thank you, Jamal, for being there when I needed you. Thank you, Mrs. Vonreyn, for teaching me MATH because (thanks to you) it is now my ... favorite subject in school. You are the best! Special thanks to Richard Spraggins for teaching me the difference between IMAGINATION and ILLUSION. However, my favorite word that you have ever taught me is ALTRUISM: - Unselfish concern for the welfare of others.

It is what inspired the idea for this book. Once again, THANK YOU!

Last but not least, I would like to thank Mr. Alfonso Garrison for never giving up on us. Love you always.

If I did not mention you in this acknowledgement, please write your name here:

_____

because I love you too!

I TOLD YOU SO

CHAPTER 1

SEE IT ALL

My name is Derrick Fluellen Jr., also known as Prince Rico, and when I was only six years old, I realized that I was smart and more advanced than the average kid who was my same age. I soon realized right from wrong and knew I had the power to make right and wrong choices. That's when I realized I was in full control. The mind controls the body, not the other way around! I also realized that everything started from a thought, allowing me to visualize my future. Yeah, even now at thirteen years old.

I'm writing this book because I'm going to be really famous one day and I plan to show you exactly how I did it. Notice that I said "I'M GOING TO BE FAMOUS," instead of saying, "I WANT TO BE FAMOUS." Wanting something is only a strong desire, kind of like a fantasy. But when you say that you are going to do something - and know that you are going to do it - then you can pretty much guarantee its money in the bank. How do I know? Because I can see it all!

Imagine that you went to Disney World. Close your eyes and "SEE" yourself in Orlando, Florida, on a nice summer afternoon, having the time of your life. Imagine or see every little detail: Who is there with you? What do things look like? Do you see Disney characters, like say, Daisy, Goofy, maybe Thumper, or even Mickey? Do the roller coasters look cool? Or do they appear to be scary?

I TOLD YOU SO

Ok, now go through the whole amusement park. Close your eyes again. Take as long as you want. See yourself doing everything at Disney World. If your parents are there with you, look at the smile on their faces, also notice the smiles on everyone else's face; feel the smile on your face. Smell the food in the air. Imagine every little detail.

This is what you call "VISUALIZING." It is being able to "SEE" something with your imagination. Visualizing things in your mind is very important because you have to "SEE" things or understand them in your mind before you can do them. It is kind of like this: Before you can really do something, you have to be able to see it in your mind or understand it first.

We understood how this process worked before we actually rode a bicycle for the first time. We understood the directions; we looked at the bike, we could "SEE" ourselves pedaling the pedals, gripping the handlebars, and going as fast as we could. In other words, we have looked at the bike and believed we could do it, then we decided how we would do it, and we could "SEE" Ourselves doing it. Then we go up to the bike and take off. Of course, most of us fell a couple of times before we actually got the hang of things, but we eventually became pros at riding a bike because we visualized it in our minds first. The same thing goes for swimming. But what happens if someone only tries to swim one try and give up? **THIS IS WHY VISUALIZING IS IMPORTANT!**

I can see myself as a very famous person in my adult future. What can you see yourself as?

CHAPTER 2

YOU CAN LEARN A LOT FROM A DUMMY

One time I heard someone say. "You can learn a lot from a dummy." That's very true because I try to do the complete opposite of what all dumb people do. For example, most dumb people are negative; that's why I stay positive because I like to consider myself as a smart, well-mannered kid. Also, most dumb people tell a lot of lies and are constantly looking for someone to mess over. The reason why I stay honest because doors are always opening up for trustworthy people. They also open to dishonest people but eventually, the dumb person burns their bridges. What would happen if a movie producer has seen a lot of potential in you, and they wanted you to star in their up-and-coming movie, but they could not trust you? EXACTLY! That's why you have to be honest at all times because opportunities may jump out at you at any given time. Here's a story about a dummy who you can learn a lot from. It's called

The Rich Man and the Builder.

CHAPTER 3

THE RICH MAN & THE BUILDER

One day a rich man approached a builder and said, "I want you to build me the best house that you can build. It is for a friend of mine who I think very highly of, so be sure to put your best skill and creativity into it. I want you to spare no expense to build the best home for my friend. Use only the best materials and workmanship. Structure it solidly, finish it elegantly, and furnish it beautifully so that I can present it to my friend with pride and confidence. I leave the details all to you. I will return when the house is complete. I will pay whatever price you feel is fair when you are done."

The builder agreed to start the project. The plans were drawn, the blueprints came to life, and construction began. As the work progressed, the builder began to see ways to save himself time and make a lot of money. No one was going to inspect the construction work, and the finish would hide it all anyway. He began to cut corners, used poor materials he got for dirt cheap and ignored some of the electrical and plumbing rules designed for safety and stability. He also bought furniture that looked good but would fade and wear & tear in a few years. He congratulated himself that by charging for the best workmanship and materials, he would make a lot of money on this project.

When the house was completed, it looked like the part -- new, elegant, a home anyone might want to live in. Only the builder knew its defects, and they probably would not show up for a few years anyway. When the rich man returned, he and the builder went together to see the house.

"My friend," said the rich man, as together they looked at the scene, "This is a fine-looking home. Now I have a surprise for you. I told you I wanted it built to give to a friend of mine. You are that friend. It was built by you and for you, and now I give it to you. It is yours. Live in it forever and enjoy it."

Trust is everything! People who are honest can always be trusted, even with big projects. Dumb people, on the other hand, do not tell the truth because they think they have the upper hand for a while. But in the end, most lies are brought to light, and people will think twice before trusting someone who has lied in the past. If you want to be famous like I will be, you have to always be honest because you never know who is paying attention to you.

Besides, it's the right thing to do!

What would this world, country, even our schools be like if everyone could trust every other person? Do you think it is possible? If so, what are you doing that will help this world become more trustworthy?

DERRICK FLUELLEN JR.

WHAT WOULD YOU DO IN EACH OF THE FOLLOWING SITUATIONS? REMEMBER, BE HONEST!

I TOLD YOU SO

A.

As soon as you got on the school bus and sat down, you noticed that someone left their cellphone next to where you are sitting. When you picked up the phone, you noticed that the screensaver was someone who made jokes about you in the past. What kind of opportunity do you see this as?

B.

You and your mom go out to eat at an expensive restaurant. She goes to the restroom before she sits down. When you sit down at the table, notice that the guy who was at the table before you and your mom left a $10.00 tip sitting on the table. The waitress is in the back, and no one can see you. What kind of opportunity do you see this as?

I TOLD YOU SO

C.

You go to Game Stop and pay for a video game that cost $35.00. You pay the desk clerk with the $50.00 bill you earned from allowances, and she gave you back a $20.00 bill. You notice right off that she gave you back too much change, but she does not. She closes the cash drawer and says, "Thank You." What kind of opportunity do you see this as?

If you are truly trying to help make this world a trustworthy place, then you should have answered:

An opportunity to do the right thing by being honest for **A, B, and C**.

Every day we have many opportunities to do the right thing, and doing the right thing will lead to success in our adult lives. But just because you helped an elderly person with their groceries does not mean that you have everything else figured out. Just like we needed to learn how to add and subtract before we could learn how to multiply and divide, it is unrealistic to think anyone can solve hard math problems without knowing the basics first.

We were taught honesty in elementary school, but if we apply it to our everyday lives and continue to **"VISUALIZE,"** we will start to understand more confusing stuff, **LIKE RELATIONSHIPS!** We will then start to learn new ideas, which will lead to success, and for me... My fame!

CHAPTER 4

BELIEVE IN YOURSELF

JAMIE FOXX

A talented singer, comedian, actor, and Academy Award winner, Jamie Foxx has proven that he is a triple threat in the entertainment world.

Jamie Foxx was born Eric Morlan Bishop on December 13, 1967, in Terrell, Texas. After his parents divorced, he was adopted by his grandparents before he turned one year old. He enjoyed sports and music as a child and went to Terrell High School in his hometown. After receiving a scholarship, he enrolled at the U.S. International University in San Diego, where he majored in music.

At the time, he was going to college when he was encouraged by some of his friends to take the open mic one night at a comedy club, and from there, his career took off.

I'm going to take my acting career serious just like Jamie Foxx did. He was serious about pursuing his dream of being an actor until he finally got his big break within Living Color. Now He's a well-known actor in the movie world. Who would have ever imagined that a simple guy from Terrell, Texas, would have made it big? I know who imagined it ... Jamie Foxx did!

Many people (unlike Jamie Fox) tell themselves negative things all day long: I won't be able to get good grades, I won't pass the test, so what's the use in trying, I know we won't win the game, etc., etc.
But this way of thinking is a huge mistake because if you tell yourself, you cannot do something; your brain believes you. That's why it's important to believe in yourself because when you do, you will accomplish wonderful things.

Businessman Warren Buffett said, "If you think you're going to succeed, you will." And Henry Ford said, "If you think you won't succeed, you won't." Instead of telling yourself all the things you can't do, tell yourself you can do great things and be a big success. Your brain will work super hard to make sure it comes true. And even if things do not work out with the first couple of tries, you can NEVER give up.

CHAPTER 5

NEVER GIVE UP

You have probably heard the saying, "If at first, you don't succeed, try again." I don't know what this saying means to you, but to me, it means to stay at what you have in mind to accomplish until it is done; to never stop, tap-out or give up. People who quit the first time they are thrown down will make a habit of quitting at the first sign of failure.

One important thing I've learned within my thirteen years on this earth is the beauty in the struggle of getting up after falling. It helps us become better people. When Thomas Edison was trying to invent the light bulb, he was interviewed by a reporter who asked him how many different ways he had tried. Thomas Edison answered, "517." The reporter said, "You mean to tell me that you failed 517 times, and you kept going?" Edison said, "I have not failed. I have positive proof that there are 517 ways that do not work. That means I am much closer to finding the way that will work."

That is very cool to me because now, today, you can look at the very same light bulb that you are using to read this book and think about Thomas Edison. Now that's what you call famous!

So even after a lot of falls and failures, becoming a pro at anything you try could happen with just a little more effort. Imagine your favorite basketball or football player, rapper, or movie star. What if that person gave up before making it big? We would never know a LeBron James, a Kobe Bryant, Tom Brady, Lil Baby, or a Denzel Washington.

DERRICK FLUELLEN JR.

"Work Hard Enough Never Give Up and Dreams Come True".... Kobe Bryant

CHAPTER 6

This is a poem, and it is called The Race. D. H. Groberg wrote it:

THE RACE

"Quit! Give up! You're beaten!" They shout at me and plead.

"There's just too much against you now.

This time you can't succeed!"

And as I start to hang my head in front of failure's face,

My downward fall is broken by the memory of a race.

DERRICK FLUELLEN JR.

A children's race, young boys, young men-
How I remember well.
Excitement, sure - But also fear. It wasn't hard to tell.

They all lined up, so full of hope. Each thought to win the race.
Or tie for first, or if not that, at least take second place.

And fathers watched off the side, each cheering for his son.
And each hoped to show his dad that he would be the one.

The whistle blew - and off they went,
Young hearts and hopes afire.
To win and be the hero was each young boy's desire.
And one boy in particular, whose dad was in the crowd,
Was running near the lead and thought to win -
"My dad will be so proud!"

But as he speeded down the field, across a shallow dip,
The little boy who thought to win lost his step and slipped.

Trying hard to catch himself, his hands flew out to brace,
And 'mid the laughter of the crowd, he fell flat on his face.

So down he fell, and with him hope - he couldn't win it now.
Embarrassed, sad, he only wished to disappear somehow.

I TOLD YOU SO

But as he fell, his dad stood up and showed his anxious face. Which to the boy so clearly said: "Get up and win the race!"

He quickly rose, no damage done, behind a bit - that's all,
And ran with all his might and mind to make up from the fall.

So anxious to restore himself - to catch up and to win -
His mind went faster than his legs - he slipped and fell again!

He wished then he had quit before, with only one disgrace.
"I'm hopeless as a runner, now. I shouldn't try to race!"

But in the laughing crowd, he searched and found his father's face. That steady look which said again, "Get up and win the race!"

So up he surged to try again - ten yards behind the last -
"If I'm to gain those yards," he thought, "I've got to move real fast."

Exerting everything he had regained eight or ten.
But trying hard to catch the lead, he slipped and fell again.
DEFEAT! He lay there silently; a tear dropped from his eye.
"There's no sense running anymore.
Three strikes - I'm out! Why try?

DERRICK FLUELLEN JR.

The will to rise had disappeared. All hope had fled away.

So far behind, so error-prone - A loser all the way.

"I've lost, so what's the use," He thought.

"I'll live with my disgrace."

But then he thought about his dad, whom soon he'd have to face.

"Get up," an echo sounded low. "Get up and take your place.

You are not meant for failure here. Get up and win the race."

"With borrowed will, get up," it said. "You haven't lost at all.

For winning is no more than this - to rise each time you fall."

So, he rose to run once more and with a new commit,

He resolved that win or lose, at least he wouldn't quit!

So far behind the others now - the most he'd ever been.

Still, he gave it all he had and ran as though to win

Three times he'd fallen, stumbling. Three times he rose again. Too far

behind to hope to win, he still ran to the end.

They cheered the winning runner,

As he crossed the line - first place.

Head high and proud and happy - no falling, no disgrace.

I TOLD YOU SO

But when the fallen youngster crossed the line - last place, the crowd gave him a greater cheer - for finishing the race.

And even though he came in last, with head held low, unproud,
You would have thought he won the race, to listen to the crowd.

And to his dad, he sadly said, "I didn't do so well."
"To me, you won," His father said, "You rose each time you fell."

And now, when things seem dark and hard and difficult to face,
The memory of that little boy helps me in my own race.

For all of life is like that race, with ups and downs and all. And all you have to do to win is rise each time you fall.

"Quit! Give up! You're beaten!" They still shout in my face.
But another voice within me says, "Get up and win the race."

CHAPTER 7

THE AVENGERS

I'm really into Marvel and the Avengers. I enjoy all the characters, their awesome images, powers, and personal history. It even blows my mind of how famous some of the characters are. It's amazing to think of how many great movies, video games, DVD's, toys, and books are based on these heroes, villains, and far-out stories, which I know the Marvel guys had so much fun creating.

Did you know that there are more than a thousand Marvel classic characters? Yep, anyone ranging from X-Men, The Incredible Hulk, Iron Man, Captain America, Thor, to even Howard The Duck - Yes, I said

I TOLD YOU SO

Howard The Duck!

But my favorite character of all time (and the one I think is the most famous) is, of course, Spider-Man. I like his image and his powers, but for the most part, I really enjoy his story.

Spider Man's real name is Peter Benjamin Parker, and his parents died in a plane crash while he was still a young kid. When they said their goodbyes at the airport, his parents told him to be a good boy for his Aunt May and Uncle Ben Parker, who later raised him as their own son. He was very close to his Uncle Ben; he even considered him as his best friend.

Peter really liked school, and he liked school so much that he became an honor student. And his teachers really liked him, but the other students had zero love for a know-it-all like puny Parker. The girls thought he was too quiet, and the boys saw him as a wimp.

One day his life changed forever. It was on the day when Peter went to a science fair by himself where he was bitten by a spider that had been exposed to a large dose of radiation. It only took Peter a few hours later to find out that he could stick to walls, and he gained other amazing powers too, like strength, speed, alertness, and reflexes like a spider. Not to mention, a

"Spider-Sense" that warned him of danger.

He was so excited about his new powers that he designed a costume that hid his identity, built a pair of web-shooters, and went into showbusiness using the Amazing Spider-Man as his stage name.

Spider-Man soon found himself battling criminals like the Chameleon, the Vulture, **DOCTOR OCTOPUS**, the **SANDMAN**, **DOCTOR DOOM**, the **LIZARD**, **ELECTRO**, **MYSTERIO**, the **GREEN GOBLIN**, the Scorpion, and many more.

I think that to be a superhero means to do good things to improve the environment. When you are doing good things, you make the world a better place because other people are watching and· learning from what you are doing. Me, myself; .by doing good things, I feel like Spider-Man because I'm doing my part in helping the world become a better place. So, when we are walking to class, working on homework, and staying positive at school, we are **ALL** improving the entire environment. So, **TOGETHER** we are the:

AVENGERS!

I TOLD YOU SO

YOU SHOULD LISTEN TO THE SONG:

- HERO -

BY THE FOO FIGHTERS

CHAPTER 8

CRABS IN A BUCKET

HERE ARE MORE SITUATIONS.

READ THEM

AND

ASK YOURSELF WHAT THEY REMIND YOU OF:

I TOLD YOU SO

A.

You were in class, taking a test, and a couple of students in front of you were cheating. One looked back at you and noticed that you were having trouble with the question that they just found the correct answer to by cheating. When he whispers the answer to you, do you write down what he said, or do you keep trying to figure it out for yourself?

B.

Would you leave or stay with friends who were making plans to steal from the corner store, even though they made fun of you or called you a coward for not wanting to steal with them?

I TOLD YOU SO

C.

You ask your teacher if you could go to the bathroom. Your teacher says yes, and when you step inside the bathroom, you see a couple of your friends in there doing drugs. When they offer you some, do you take part in it, or do you walk away?

All of these situations are examples of peer pressure. Something that we - as teens - face almost every day. But if you are making plans to be famous or successful in life like I plan to, you have to make your own decisions. Negative people always notice when you are doing good things with your life, so they will try to bring you back down with them. That's why it called ...... **CRABS IN A BUCKET!**

Crabs kinda look like lobsters because, likewise, they both have four pairs of legs, an outer shell, and pincers. But if you put a bunch of crabs in one bucket - **READY TO COOK THEM** - they will, by nature, turn into evil little creatures. Instead of working together to get out of the bucket, they will bring the one who made it furthest to the edge of the top back down with them.

When people around you are doing something wrong and want you to do the same thing, don't give in. When others pressure you, you can still control the situation by making the right decision. Like, some people might tell you that trying drugs will make you feel lit or that stealing will make you popular and cool, but they are wrong. I'm pretty sure that all they really want is for you to stay at the bottom with them.

CRABS IN A BUCKET

When you put one crab in a bucket, the crab can easily escape.

When you put more than one crab in a bucket, the crabs cannot escape anymore; wherever · one tries to escape, the others will catch him and pull him back down.

It is so bad that you don't even have to put a lid on the bucket that's full of crabs - because even though each one has the ability to escape, the other's (who also has the ability to escape) will never let anyone escape.

They'll grab each other, and they'll grab the crabs trying to escape and will pull them in.

Basically, the crab in a bucket mentality is the mentality where they are HATERS who won't let you get ahead because of jealousy or people who want to compete with you.

You HAVE to be the crab that escapes.

You HAVE to rise to the top, above the haters.

How do I escape the crab bucket of haters?

Continue doing good things, stay positive, and do not care what anyone thinks or has to say about it!

CHAPTER 9

MAKE A TURNAROUND LIKE JUSTIN BIEBER

Hopefully, by now, you can see that what I am trying to say is that with positive energy, we - meaning all of us - can become famous or anything that we set ourselves out to be. What we "THINK" is what we will become! I read that people think around 50,000 thoughts each day. WOW, now that's a lot of thinking! But our thoughts can be positive or negative; it's all up to us. Only you and I can choose how we think about our future and what happens to us in our lives.

True, we can never know what might happen next, but if we think and act positively, we can triple ours. Chances of having great lives. Even if you make mistakes or start negative, you can always make a turnaround like Justin Bieber did.

JUSTIN BIEBER

Justine Bieber is a Canadian singer and songwriter. He was born in 1994 in Stratford, Ontario, Canada, to a single mom. Justine Bieber took second place in a local talent show at a young age. After his mom posted a YouTube video of her son performing, Bieber went from an unknown, untrained singer to a **MEGA SUPERSTAR** with a big-time record deal with Usher. He became the first solo artist to have four singles enter the top 40 before the release of a dept album. His 2009 album, My World, went platinum in several countries. He later experienced a lot of media attention because of his negative behavior.

Surviving public scandals, lawsuits, and more than a few arrests for bad behavior, Justine Bieber made an awesome turnaround after admitting that he was battling depression. That's when he decided to clean up his act. In

March of 2019, he posted a picture on Instagram of himself praying with Kanye West:

"Just wanted to keep you guys updated a little bit. Hopefully, what I'm going through will resonate with you guys. Been struggling a lot. Just feeling super disconnected and weird. I always bounce back, so I'm not worried, just wanted to reach out and ask for you guys to pray for me. God is faithful, and your prayers worked, ... Thanks, the most human season I've ever been in, facing my stuff head-on."

While facing his problems with a new and positive attitude, Justin Bieber is now happily married with a long-lasting future ahead of himself.

DERRICK FLUELLEN JR.

YOU SHOULD LISTEN TO JUSTIN BIEBER'S SONG:

"HOLY"

FT. CHANCE THE RAPPER

I TOLD YOU SO

CHAPTER 10

PRACTICE MAKES PERFECT

Have you ever heard of Helen Keller? If you are not sure who she was, she lived from 1880 to 1968, and before she turned two years old, she lost her eyesight and hearing. By the time she was a teenager, she was unable to talk. But her teacher, Anne Sullivan, helped her overcome her disabilities. It wasn't easy, though! Helen made many mistakes at first while Anne was trying to teach her how to communicate. Why? Because this was something new to Helen. But with a lot of practice (and Anne never giving up on her), Helen not only learned how to communicate, but she also became an author. Then Helen Keller went on to help other people who had problems like her own. Now to this day, her story is talked about all over the world. You should watch her movie, "The Miracle Worker."

Whenever you try something new, 9 times out of 10, you will make many mistakes. Like, remember the hard math problems that I was talking about? Especially if it's a math problem that you never even seen before; you will probably make many mistakes at first. But if you stick with it, you will eventually solve it with ease. Even trying a new sport, you will probably need to spend a lot of time practicing the basics before you are really good.

I TOLD YOU SO

I have been playing football since the 5th grade. Now that I am in the In 8th grade, I play football for the Pittsburg Pirates. When I first started playing, I was horrible (on top of being small), so people underestimated me. But with a lot of practice and believing in myself, I got really good at it. Now I play offense and defense because my coach noticed that my skills were getting a lot better. My proudest moment was when my mom was at one of my games, and she witnessed me make a huge tackle. Let's just say that the practicing really paid off!

Do not be scared of trying new things because choosing not to do something new (that requires a lot of practice) is like sitting around waiting and doing the same old, lame stuff all the time ...... And that's really boring! When I become famous, I'm going to show you that by trying something new and with a lot of practice, anything is possible.

CHAPTER 11

SHOOTING FOR THE STARS

A star is any of the luminous celestial objects seen as a light way up in the sky. Although they are over several hundred of thousand miles away, stars still shine bright on us, here down on earth. To be a star, you have to cast back positive light, to those who are looking up to you. To be a star means **DREAM BIG** because small dreams do not have to power like a celestial star to move people.

Huge dreams are ideas that motivate people to do amazing things. They are dreams so big that they are powerful, like a star to move people. Huge dreams also help people see that **IMPOSSIBLE** can really happen with positive energy, never giving up, believing in yourself, and seeing it all.

I will fill you in on a little secret. When you say that you are going to do something and **KNOW** that you are going to do it, the whole universe works together in helping you do it. Think about that for a while. In the meantime, I will see you amongst the stars. This book was just one small example of the unlimited ways of me saying:

I TOLD YOU SO!

I TOLD YOU SO

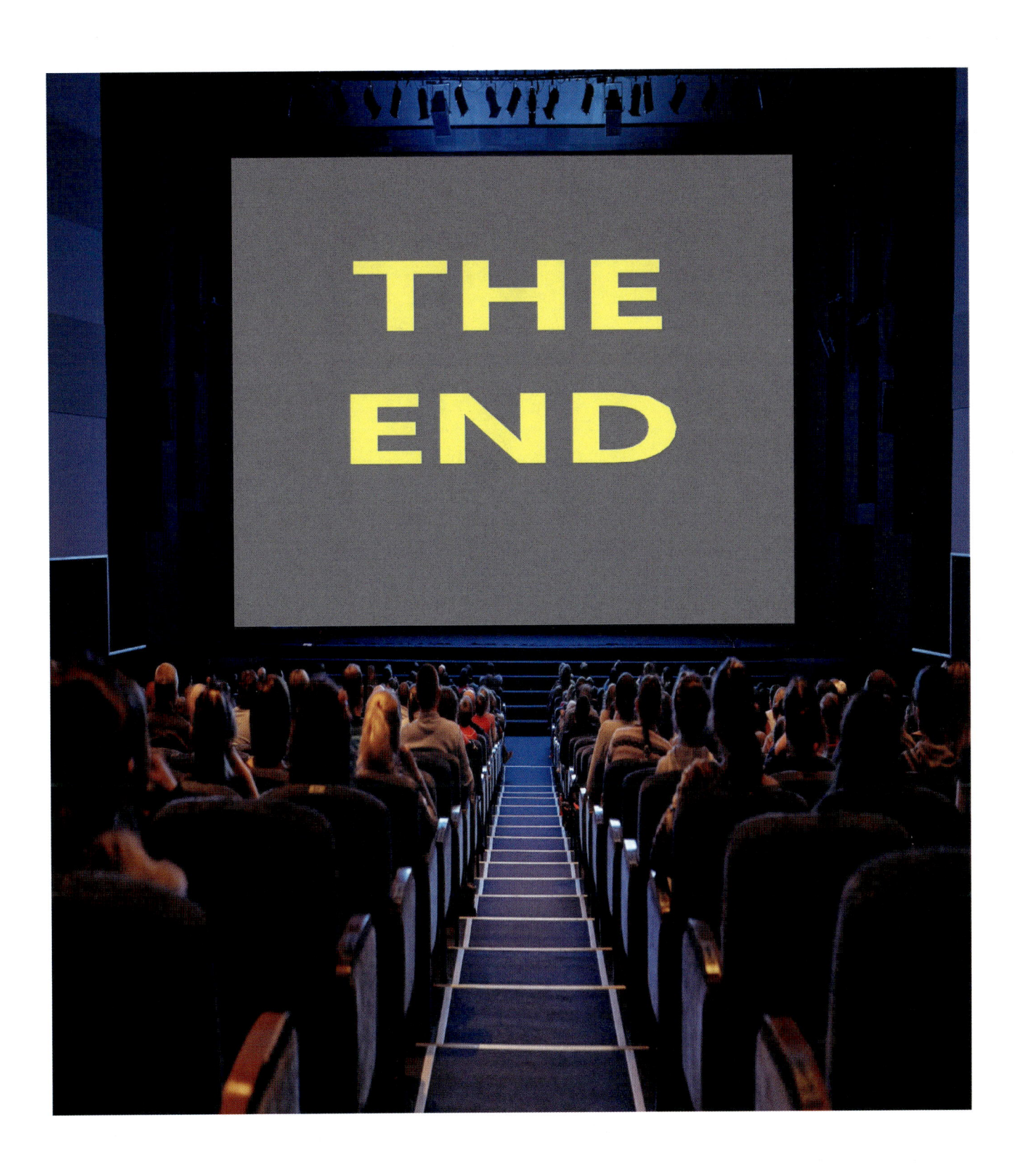

DERRICK FLUELLEN JR.

ABOUT THE AUTHOR

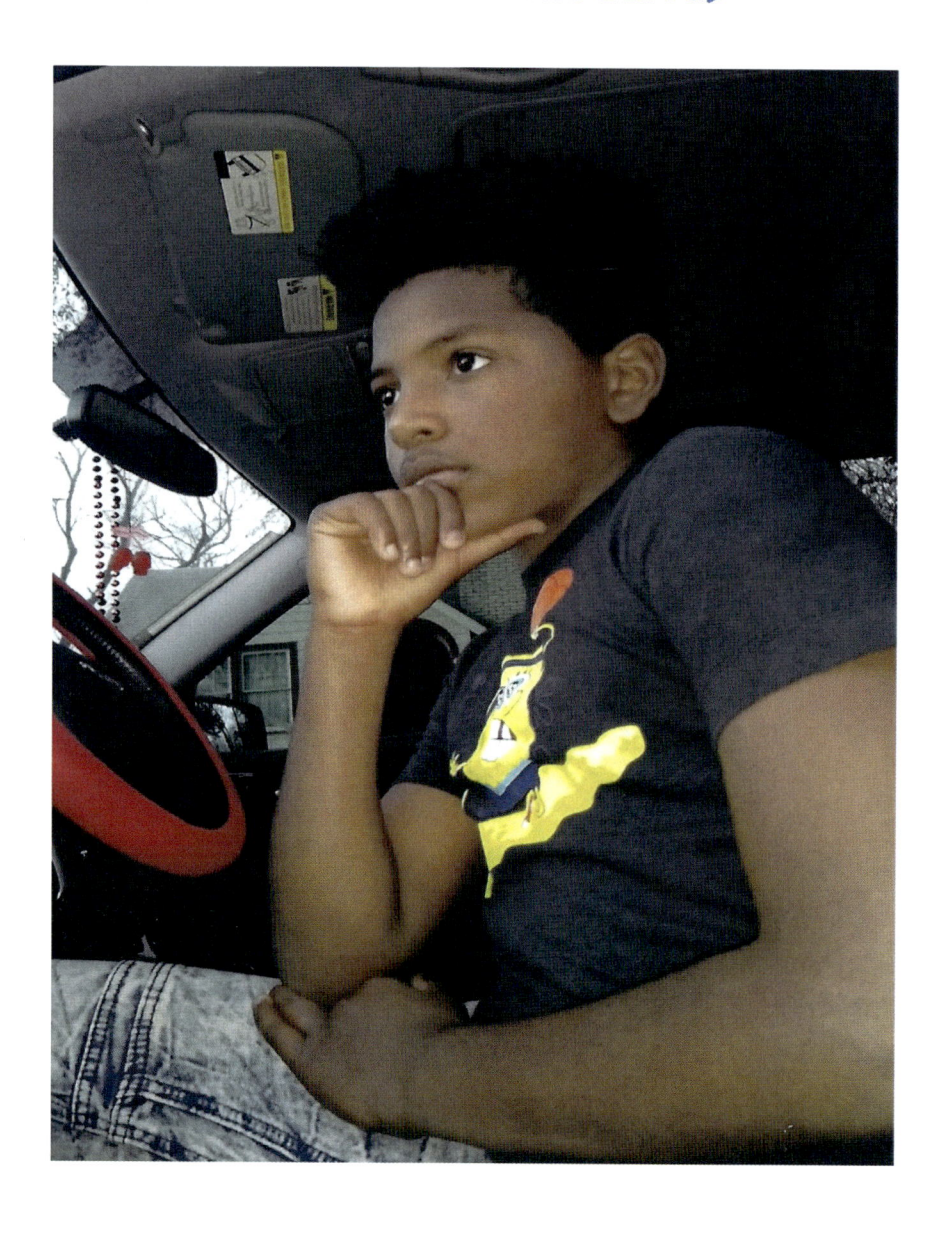

Derrick Fluellen Jr. is an aspiring actor who currently attends Pittsburg Jr. High School in Pittsburg, Texas. His favorite pastimes include watching Anime, larping, playing Minecraft, dancing, singing, and collecting Pokémon cards. Likewise, he loves to watch the tv show Ben 10.

While the average teen avoids the notion of math and complex equations,

I TOLD YOU SO

it's Derrick's favorite subject in school. Besides, it's apparent and universally understood that Derrick Fluellen Jr. is by far from the average teenager. This Child Prodigy has extraordinary potential who knows exactly where he's headed and how he's going to get there. We here at Free To Create Publications attest (just like you should) that he's a surefire to success, fame, and anything else that he's determined to be.

PITTSBURG JUNIOR HIGH SCHOOL
Interim Progress Report
As of December 07, 2020 11:01

Student Name	Student ID	Grade Level	Semester
FLUELLEN, DERRICK O	014338	08	1

Course	Period	Teacher	Curr Avg	Ovr Avg	Cycle Abs Exc	Cycle Abs Un	Cycle Abs Sch	Comment Codes
0982 CHOIR 8	01 - 01	KODER, MARY	100		1	0	0	
0581 SCIENCE 8	02 - 02	HALL, SONYA	095		0	1	0	
0181 BOYS' ATH 8	03 - 03	STYLES, CHRISTOPHER	100		0	0	0	
0381 MATH 8	04 - 05	VONREYN, RACHEL	100		0	0	0	
0681 SOCIAL ST 8	06 - 06	WRIGHT, MELODY	099		0	0	0	
0483 ELAR 8	07 - 08	VICKERS, GLADYS	097		0	1	0	

PUBLISHER'S NOTES:

The Benefits of Theater Arts and Acting School are:

Arts are such an important part of children's lives. This encompasses not only dancing and singing but also acting. Drama improves a child's public speaking skills. Talking and performing in front of audiences will teach children so many important parts of public speaking, including volume, pronunciation, and inflection. Acting increases a teamwork mentality because when working with a cast, a child is put into a team environment where everyone matters and has a part. This builds a teamwork mentality that can't even compare to group projects. Drama improves a child's confidence because being on stage is not for the light of heart. You perform in front of strangers, and this, in turn, makes your child more confident and able to handle the most embarrassing situations that can arise. Acting makes a child more physically active. As you know, many kids decide at an early age that sports aren't for them. Performing, on the other hand, can be a good alternative to physical activity. Between dance choreography, blocking during rehearsal, building sets, or just wasting time with fellow actors, acting gets a child moving. Performing in plays increases memorization, insomuch that when learning lines, blocking, cues, and lighting, actors use many memorization tricks to remember everything. These tricks follow performers throughout their life while helping with studying in school and multitasking at work. For the most part, being in drama and on stage improves professionalism. For a lot of children, the theater is the beginning of professional behavior. When in the dramatic arts, children have to make a great impression on directors, support fellow actors, show enthusiasm, work hard, and treat everyone equally. This follows through into a child's work and professional life. Therefore – with that said – all proceeds of this book will go towards Derrick Fluellen's aspiration to attend Theater Arts and Acting School.

A beautiful mind is a terrible thing to waste!

Made in the USA
Columbia, SC
03 February 2022